S0-ANF-102

A Treasury of Days

365 Thoughts on the Art of Living

A Treasury of Days

365 Thoughts on the Art of Living

EDITED BY DEE DANNER BARWICK

A READER'S DIGEST/C.R.GIBSON BOOK

Published by The C.R. Gibson Company, Norwalk, Connecticut 06856

The acknowledgments that appear on pages 92-95 are hereby made a part of this copyright page.

A Reader's Digest/C.R.Gibson book published by arrangement with The Reader's Digest Association, Inc., Pleasantville, N.Y., 10570.

Printed in the United States of America.

ISBN: 0-8378-1803-6

Perhaps the best reason for having calendars and for marking life in years is that the cycle itself offers hope. We need fresh starts and new chances, the conviction that beginnings remain available, no matter how many we've blown. And the yearly clock can start anywhere along the line.

LOUDON WAINWRIGHT

January

1

Be at war with your vices, at peace with your neighbors, and let every new year find you a better person.

BENJAMIN FRANKLIN

2

Begin at once to live, and count each day as a separate life.

LUCIUS ANNAEUS SENECA

3

I have always been delighted at the prospect of a new day, a fresh try, one more start, with perhaps a bit of magic waiting somewhere behind the morning.

J. B. PRIESTLEY

4

If I were to wish for anything, I should not wish for wealth and power but for the passionate sense of the potential, for the eye which, ever young and ardent, sees the possible. Pleasure disappoints, possibility never. And what wine is so sparkling, what so fragrant, what so intoxicating, as possibility!

SÖREN KIERKEGAARD

5

Lady Luck has been good to me. I fancy she has been good to many. Only some people are dour, and when she gives them the come-hither with her eyes, they look down or turn away. But me — I give her the wink, and away we go.

WILLIAM ALLEN WHITE

6

If I were to begin life again, I should want it as it was. I would only open my eyes a little more.

JULES RENARD

7

You can't turn back the clock. But you can wind it up again.

BONNIE PRUDDEN

8

Sometimes when you are feeling jaded or blasé, you can revive your sense of wonder by merely saying to yourself:

Suppose this were the only time. Suppose this sunset, this moonrise, this symphony, this buttered toast, this sleeping child, this flag against the sky . . . suppose you would never experience these things again!

Few things are commonplace in themselves. It's our reaction to them that grows dull, as we move forward through the years.

ARTHUR GORDON

9

An open mind collects more riches than an open purse.

WILL HENRY

10

There are four mental types among human beings:

The man who knows, and is aware that he knows: he is wise, so inquire of him.

The man who knows, but is unaware that he knows: remind him and help him that he forget not.

The man who is ignorant, and knows that he is ignorant: teach him.

The man who is ignorant, but pretends to know: he is a fool, so keep away from him.

SOLOMON IBN GABIROL

11

People are like stained-glass windows; they sparkle and shine when the sun is out, but when the darkness sets in, their true beauty is revealed only if there is a light from within.

ELIZABETH KÜBLER-ROSS

12

One ought every day to hear a little music, read a good poem, see a fine picture and, if possible, speak a few reasonable words.

JOHANN WOLFGANG VON GOETHE

13

"Tell me what you read and I'll tell you who you are" is true enough, but I'd know you better if you told me what you reread.

FRANÇOIS MAURIAC

14

Cato the Elder, on observing statues being set up in honor of others, remarked: "I would rather have people ask 'Why isn't there a statue to Cato?' than 'Why is there one?' "

THOMAS L. MASSON

15

What great thing would you attempt if you knew you could not fail?

ROBERT H. SCHULLER

16

I find the great thing in this world is not so much where we stand as in what direction we are moving. To reach the port of heaven, we must sail sometimes with the wind and sometimes against it—but we must sail, and not drift, nor lie at anchor.

OLIVER WENDELL HOLMES

17

He who never made a mistake never made a discovery.

SAMUEL SMILES

18

To err is human; to blame it on the other guy is even more human.

BOB GODDARD

19

Admit your own mistakes openly, maybe even joyfully. Encourage your associates to do likewise by commiserating with them. Never castigate. Babies learn to walk by falling down. If you beat a baby every time he falls down, he'll never care much for walking.

ROBERT TOWNSEND

20

The only nice thing about being imperfect is the joy it brings to others.

DOUG LARSON

21

There are two insults no human being will endure: that he has no sense of humor, and that he has never known trouble.

SINCLAIR LEWIS

22

After the ship has sunk, everyone knows how it might have been saved.

ITALIAN PROVERB

23

Life is like playing a violin solo in public and learning the instrument as one goes on.

SAMUEL BUTLER

24

The great secret known to internists, but still hidden from the general public, is that most things get better by themselves. Most things, in fact, are better by morning.

LEWIS THOMAS

25

There is nothing final about a mistake, except its being taken as final.

PHYLLIS BOTTOME

26

Make it a rule of life never to regret and never to look back. Regret is an appalling waste of energy; you can't build on it; it's only good for wallowing in.

KATHERINE MANSFIELD

27

If it's true the mind is like a sponge, I wish I could squeeze mine out once in a while and get rid of stuff I don't need anymore.

BERYL PFIZER

28

Times like these, it helps to recall that there have always *been times like these.*

PAUL HARVEY

29

We act as though comfort and luxury were the chief requirements of life, when all that we need to make us really happy is something to be enthusiastic about.

CHARLES KINGSLEY

30

Enthusiasm is the thing that makes the world go round. Without its driving power nothing worth doing has ever been done. It alleviates the pains of poverty and the boredom of riches. Apart from it joy cannot live. Therefore, it should be husbanded with zeal and spent with wisdom. To waste it is folly; to misuse it, disaster.

ROBERT HAVEN SCHAUFFLER

31

I prefer the errors of enthusiasm to the indifference of wisdom.

ANATOLE FRANCE

February

1

The art of living consists in knowing which impulses to obey and which must be made to obey.

SYDNEY J. HARRIS

2

It is possible to skim the surface of life without being profoundly touched by anything, but it's not very rewarding. Those who close themselves off from pain must also sacrifice opportunities to feel a piercing sense of joy. To feel deeply, to know the fullest dimensions of ourselves and others, we must feel everything.

EDA LESHAN

3

Anyone can carry his burden, however hard, until nightfall. Anyone can do his work, however hard, for one day. Anyone can live sweetly, patiently, lovingly, purely, till the sun goes down. And this is all that life really means.

ROBERT LOUIS STEVENSON

4

I have lived in this world just long enough to look carefully the second time into things that I am the most certain of the first time.

JOSH BILLINGS

5

If in the last few years you haven't discarded a major opinion or acquired a new one, check your pulse. You may be dead.

GELETT BURGESS

6

The subconscious mind is the fireless cooker where our ideas simmer while we are loafing. Newton was loafing when he saw an apple fall and got the gravitation idea. While finding peace for his soul, Galileo watched the great swinging lamp. It gave him the idea of the pendulum swinging to and fro as a means of measuring the passage of time. Watt was relaxing in the kitchen when he saw steam lifting the top of the teakettle and conceived the idea of a steam engine.

Many times we will get more and better ideas in two hours of creative loafing than in eight hours at a desk.

WILFERD A. PETERSON

7

I am always ready to learn, although I do not always like being taught.

SIR WINSTON CHURCHILL

8

Grow angry slowly—there's plenty of time.

RALPH WALDO EMERSON

9

He who's always blowing a fuse is usually in the dark.

FRANKLIN P. JONES

10

When you run into someone who is disagreeable to others, you may be sure he is uncomfortable with himself; the amount of pain we inflict upon others is directly proportional to the amount we feel within us.

SYDNEY J. HARRIS

11

When we put ourselves in the other person's place, we're less likely to want to put him in his place.

FARMER'S DIGEST

12

If you really want the last word in an argument, try saying, "I guess you're right."

FUNNY FUNNY WORLD

13

Anyone can become angry. That is easy. But to be angry with the right person, to the right degree, at the right time, for the right purpose and in the right way—that is not easy.

ARISTOTLE

14

You can tell more about a person by what he says about others than you can by what others say about him.

LEO AIKMAN

15

When you ask from a stranger that which is of interest only to yourself, always enclose a stamp.

ABRAHAM LINCOLN

16

The greatest pleasure I know is to do a good action by stealth and have it found out by accident.

CHARLES LAMB

17

The shortest and surest way to live with honor in the world is to be in reality what we appear to be.

SOCRATES

18

There are two statements about human beings that are true: that all human beings are alike, and that all are different. On those two facts all human wisdom is founded.

MARK VAN DOREN

19

If you have anything valuable to contribute to the world, it will come through the expression of your own personality—that single spark of divinity that sets you off and makes you different from every other living creature.

BRUCE BARTON

20

He who walks in another's tracks leaves no footprints.

JOAN L. BRANNON

21

We all live under the same sky, but we don't all have the same horizon.

KONRAD ADENAUER

22

Far better it is to dare mighty things, to win glorious triumphs, even though checkered by failure, than to take rank with those poor spirits who neither enjoy much nor suffer much, because they live in the gray twilight that knows not victory nor defeat.

THEODORE ROOSEVELT

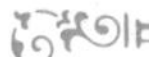

23

Challenges make you discover things about yourself that you never really knew. They're what make the instrument stretch—what make you go beyond the norm.

CICELY TYSON

24

When you are exasperated by interruptions, try to remember that their very frequency may indicate the valuableness of your life. Only the people who are full of help and strength are burdened by other people's needs. The interruptions which we chafe at are the credentials of our indispensability. The greatest condemnation that anybody could incur—and it is a danger to guard against—is to be so independent, so unhelpful, that nobody ever interrupts us and we are left comfortably alone.

THE REV. CANON M.A. HUGHES—*DIALOGUE*

25

He that wrestles with us strengthens our nerves and sharpens our skill. Our antagonist is our helper.

EDMUND BURKE

26

Most of the shadows of this life are caused by our standing in our own sunshine.

RALPH WALDO EMERSON

27

Luck is what happens when preparation meets opportunity.

ELMER G. LETERMAN

28

There is nothing noble in being superior to some other man. True nobility is being superior to your former self.

HINDU PROVERB

29

Of all the people you will know in a lifetime, you are the only one you will never leave or lose. To the question of your life, you are the only answer. To the problems of your life, you are the only solution.

FREDELLE MAYNARD

March

1

If you would find happiness, "Don't judge yourself. Accept yourself and move on from there."

MILDRED NEWMAN AND
BERNARD BERKOWITZ WITH
JEAN OWEN

2

All anybody needs to know about prizes is that Mozart never won one.

HENRY MITCHELL

3

It is easy in the world to live after the world's opinion; it is easy in solitude to live after our own; but the great man is he who in the midst of the crowd keeps with perfect sweetness the independence of solitude.

RALPH WALDO EMERSON

4

That person proves his worth who can make us want to listen when he is with us and think when he is gone.

GRIT

5

Once I had occasion to buy a silver soup ladle. The obliging salesman brought forth quite an array of them, including ultimately one that was as plain and unadorned as the unclouded sky—and about as beautiful. But the price! It was nearly double any of the others.

"You see," the salesman explained, "in this highly ornamental ware the flaws don't show. This plain one has to be the very best. Any defect would be apparent."

There, if you please, is a final basis of comparison of all things: the bare dignity of the unadorned that may stand before the world all unashamed, in the consciousness of perfection.

FRANK NORRIS

6

Beware of the fellow student or faculty member who gives himself out as a person of large importance; in the words of Van Wyck Brooks, "Genius and virtue are to be more often found clothed in gray than in peacock bright." It takes an immense amount of energy to keep up the appearance of greatness—more, indeed, than the great are prepared to give.

DR. ALEXANDER G. BEARN

7

What really matters is what happens in us, not to us.

THE REV. JAMES W. KENNEDY

8

Watch your thoughts, they become words;
watch your words, they become actions;
watch your actions, they become habits;
watch your habits, they become character;
watch your character, for it becomes your destiny.

FRANK OUTLAW

9

Many people believe that admitting a fault means they no longer have to correct it.

MARIE VON EBNER-ESCHENBACH

10

If a small thing has the power to make you angry, does that not indicate something about your size?

SYDNEY J. HARRIS

11

All blame is a waste of time. No matter how much fault you find with another, and regardless of how much you blame him, it will not change you. The only thing blame does is to keep the focus off you when you are looking for external reasons to explain your unhappiness or frustration. You may succeed in making another feel guilty of something by blaming him, but you won't succeed in changing whatever it is about you that is making you unhappy.

WAYNE W. DYER

12

Fate is what life gives to you. Destiny is what you do with it. If you are five-four, you ain't ever going to be six-two. If you have trouble putting the cap on your toothpaste tube in the morning, mechanical engineering is not for you.

That's fate.

But the way a person accepts the things he can't change and then goes 105 percent for the things he can, that's destiny. What most people tend to forget is that we have unbelievable control over our destiny.

BILL GOVE

13

The world is before you, and you need not take it or leave it as it was when you came in.

JAMES BALDWIN

14

If you want something very, very badly, let it go free. If it comes back to you, it's yours forever. If it doesn't, it was never yours to begin with.

JESS LAIR

15

Live in the active voice, not the passive. Think more about what you make happen than about what happens to you.

WILLIAM DEWITT HYDE

16

David Livingstone, the great explorer and Christian pioneer, wrote in one magnificent sentence, "I will go anywhere—provided it be forward."

WALTER RUSSELL BOWIE

17

Those who fail in life often pursue the path of least persistence.

DUBOIS COUNTY, IND., *HERALD*

18

Never confuse motion with action.

ERNEST HEMINGWAY

19

The mind is everything; what you think, you become.

BUDDHA

20

Be yourself. No one can ever tell you you're doing it wrong.

JAMES LEO HERLIHY

21

Since God made us to be originals, why stoop to be a copy?

THE REV. BILLY GRAHAM

22

Strange how much you've got to know before you know how little you know.

DUNCAN STUART

23

Some people think it's holding on that makes one strong. Sometimes it's letting go.

SYLVIA ROBINSON

24

He approaches nearest to the gods who knows how to be silent, even though he is in the right.

CATO

25

Silence is the unbearable repartee.

G. K. CHESTERTON

26

Blessed are they who have nothing to say and who cannot be persuaded to say it.

JAMES RUSSELL LOWELL

27

Words must surely be counted among the most powerful drugs man ever invented.

LEO ROSTEN

28

If you would be pungent, be brief; for it is with words as with sunbeams. The more they are condensed, the deeper they burn.

ROBERT SOUTHEY

29

A problem well stated is a problem half solved.

CHARLES F. KETTERING

30

We may be willing to tell a story twice but we are never willing to hear it more than once.

WILLIAM HAZLITT

31

Everybody is ignorant, only on different subjects.

WILL ROGERS

April

1

No one is ever old enough to know better.

HOLBROOK JACKSON

2

The older I get, the more wisdom I find in the ancient rule of taking first things first—a process which often reduces the most complex human problems to manageable proportions.

DWIGHT D. EISENHOWER

3

Maturity is the ability to do a job whether or not you are supervised, to carry money without spending it and to bear an injustice without wanting to get even.

ANN LANDERS

4

It is very easy to forgive others their mistakes; it takes more grit and gumption to forgive them for having witnessed your own.

JESSAMYN WEST

5

He who seeks only for applause from without has all his happiness in another's keeping.

OLIVER GOLDSMITH

6

No matter what looms ahead, if you can eat today, enjoy the sunlight today, mix good cheer with friends today, enjoy it and bless God for it. Do not look back on happiness—or dream of it in the future. You are only sure of today; do not let yourself be cheated out of it.

HENRY WARD BEECHER

7

Be pleasant until ten o'clock in the morning, and the rest of the day will take care of itself.

ELBERT HUBBARD

8

We all know a fool when we see one—but not when we are one.

ARNOLD H. GLASOW

9

Our wisdom comes from our experience, and our experience comes from our foolishness.

SACHA GUITRY

10

Resisting temptation is easier when you think you'll probably get another chance later on.

BOB TALBERT

11

Faced with the choice between changing one's mind and proving that there is no need to do so, almost everyone gets busy on the proof.

JOHN KENNETH GALBRAITH

12

No one so thoroughly appreciates the value of constructive criticism as the one who's giving it.

HAL CHADWICK

13

A bore is someone who persists in holding his own views after we have enlightened him with ours.

MALCOLM S. FORBES

14

We often pardon those who bore us, but we cannot pardon those whom we bore.

LA ROCHEFOUCAULD

15

Success is knowing the difference between cornering people and getting them in your corner.

BILL COPELAND

16

People who tell you never to let little things bother you have never tried sleeping in a room with a mosquito.

KATHERINE CHANDLER

17

People may doubt what you say, but they will believe what you do.

LEWIS CASS

18

Blessed is he who has learned to admire but not envy, to follow but not imitate, to praise but not flatter, and to lead but not manipulate.

WILLIAM ARTHUR WARD

19

No person can be a great leader unless he takes genuine joy in the successes of those under him.

W. A. NANCE

20

A nation reveals itself not only by the men it produces but also by the men it honors, the men it remembers.

JOHN F. KENNEDY

21

A leader is best
when people barely know he exists.
Not so good
when people obey and acclaim him.
Worse when they despise him.
But of a good leader
who talks little
when his work is done
his aim fulfilled
they will say:
"We did it ourselves."

LAO-TSE

22

I believe that one of the most important conditioners for a real democrat with a small "d" is for him to be at some time or other exposed to adversity. It has been my experience that if a man does not suffer adversity, he never appreciates what it is like for people who do suffer it. When a fellow has been through adversity, he is more likely to have a kindlier feeling than those who have never been through trouble.

HARRY S. TRUMAN

23

I don't want men of experience working for me. The experienced man is always telling me why something can't be done; he thinks he knows the answers. The fellow who has not had any experience doesn't know a thing can't be done—and he goes ahead and does it.

CHARLES F. KETTERING

24

When someone is convinced that things can't be done, he will cling to that conviction in the face of the most obvious contradiction. At the time that Robert Fulton gave the first public demonstration of his steamboat, one of those "can't be done" fellows stood in the crowd along the shore repeating, "He can't start her."

Suddenly there was a belch of steam and the boat began to move. Startled, the man stared for a moment and then began to chant, "He can't stop her."

THE BETTER WAY

25

The impossible is often the untried.

JIM GOODWIN

26

We couldn't conceive of a miracle if none had ever happened.

LIBBIE FUDIM

27

Nothing in life is to be feared. It is only to be understood.

MARIE CURIE

28

Childhood and genius have the same master-organ in common—inquisitiveness.

E. G. BULWER-LYTTON

29

It is as much a presumption to think you can do nothing as to think there is some critical place which just you and no one else is made to fill. The latter folly supposes that God exhausted himself when he made you; the former folly, equally impious, supposes that God made a hopeless blunder when he made you.

PHILLIPS BROOKS

30

Just remember—when you think all is lost, the future remains.

BOB GODDARD

May

1

However dark it seems today, however dark it is, we shall meet life better if we have fulfilled the present to the best of our ability. Today is still ours, along with the obligation to live it to the full.

DOROTHY VAN DOREN

2

May is such a nice month—you wouldn't think it would have Mondays.

CHARLES BARSOTTI

3

It is not doing the thing we like to do, but liking the thing we have to do, that makes life blessed.

JOHANN WOLFGANG VON GOETHE

4

The good life exists only when you stop wanting a better one. It is the condition of savoring what is, rather than longing for what might be.

MARYA MANNES

5

One of the most tragic things I know about human nature is that all of us tend to put off living. We are all dreaming of some magical rose garden over the horizon —instead of enjoying the roses that are blooming outside our windows today.

DALE CARNEGIE

6

The business of living is joy in the real sense of the word, not just something for pleasure, amusement, recreation. The business of living is the celebration of being alive.

CHRISTIAAN N. BARNARD, M.D.

7

If I were to join a circle of any kind it would be a circle that required its members to try something new at least once a month. The new thing could be very inconsequential: steak for breakfast, frog hunting, walking on stilts, memorizing a stanza of poetry. It could be staying up outdoors all night, making up a dance and dancing it, speaking to a stranger, chinning yourself, milking a goat—anything not ordinarily done.

JESSAMYN WEST

8

If I had my life to live over, I'd pick more daisies.

DON HEROLD

9

There is much in life that doesn't have to be done instantly. There are phone calls that don't have to be returned immediately. There are many difficult problems and decisions that actually improve when they are left to simmer a little while.

The rhythm of life is intricate but orderly, tenacious but fragile. To keep that in mind is to hold the key to survival.

JUDGE SHIRLEY M. HUFSTEDLER

10

Life is not a 100-yard dash, but more a cross-country run. If we sprint all the time, we not only fail to win the race, but never even last long enough to reach the finish line.

JOSEPH A. KENNEDY

11

Nothing makes it easier to resist temptation than a proper bringing-up, a sound set of values—and witnesses.

FRANKLIN P. JONES

12

The truly free person is one who knows how to decline a dinner invitation without giving an excuse.

JULES RENARD

13

The genius of communication is the ability to be both totally honest and totally kind at the same time.

JOHN POWELL

14

Beware of the conversationalist who adds "in other words." He is merely starting afresh.

ROBERT MORLEY

15

A good listener is not only popular everywhere, but after a while he knows something.

WILSON MIZNER

16

Smart is when you believe only half of what you hear. Brilliant is when you know which half to believe.

ORBEN'S CURRENT COMEDY

17

Listening to both sides of a story will convince you that there is more to a story than both sides.

FRANK TYGER

18

Courage is what it takes to stand up and speak; courage is also what it takes to sit down and listen.

QUOTATIONS OF COURAGE AND VISION

19

Courage is the art of being the only one who knows you're scared to death.

EARL WILSON

20

What is more mortifying than to feel that you have missed the plum for want of courage to shake the tree?

LOGAN PEARSALL SMITH

21

No one can be completely relaxed. Like a windup clock, a person can't tick without some tension.

JOHN RAUDONIS

22

I do believe one ought to face facts. If you don't they get behind you and may become terrors, nightmares, giants, horrors. As long as one faces them one is top dog. The trouble is not to steel oneself but to face them calmly, easily—to have the habit of facing them.

KATHERINE MANSFIELD

23

My Mother, God bless her, taught me when I was little never to carry yesterday on my back. It didn't matter what had happened—yesterday was dead. I remember her saying: "There's nothing you can do about it now. If you get in the habit of carrying yesterday around on your back, you'll be bent double by the time you're 21."

DANNY THOMAS

24

My mother drew a distinction between achievement and success. She said that "achievement is the knowledge that you have studied and worked hard and done the best that is in you. Success is being praised by others, and that's nice, too, but not as important or satisfying. Always aim for achievement and forget about success."

HELEN HAYES

25

Success does not necessarily mean that we must earn a great deal of money and live in the biggest house in town. It means only that we are daily engaged in striving toward a goal that we have independently chosen and feel is worthy of us as persons. A goal, whatever it may be, is what gives meaning to our existence. It is the carrot on the stick that keeps us striving—that keeps us interested—that gives us a reason for getting out of bed in the morning.

EARL NIGHTINGALE

26

Success is how you collect your minutes. You spend millions of minutes to reach one triumph, one moment, then you spend maybe a thousand minutes enjoying it. If you were unhappy through those millions of minutes, what good are the thousands of minutes of triumph? It doesn't equate.

NORMAN LEAR

27

Time is the coin of your life. It is the only coin you have, and only you can determine how it will be spent. Be careful lest you let other people spend it for you.

CARL SANDBURG

28

Dost thou love life? Then do not squander Time, for that's the stuff Life is made of.

BENJAMIN FRANKLIN

29

However diverse their talents, temperaments and differences, all great achievers have one trait in common: They never bother to compare themselves with others, but are content to run their own race on their own terms.

SYDNEY J. HARRIS

30

If my mind can conceive it, and my heart can believe it, I know I can achieve it.

THE REV. JESSE JACKSON

31

Part of the art of living is knowing how to compare yourself with the right people. Dissatisfaction is often the result of unsuitable comparison.

DR. HEINRICH SOBOTKA

June

1

Risk is essential. There is no growth or inspiration in staying within what is safe and comfortable. Once you find out what you do best, why not try something else?

ALEX NOBLE

2

The difference in actual skill and ability and intelligence between those who succeed and those who fail is usually neither wide nor striking. But if men are nearly equally matched, the man who is enthusiastic will find the scales tipped in his favor. And the man of second-rate ability with enthusiasm will often outstrip one of first-rate ability without enthusiasm. Primarily, enthusiasm means believing in your work and loving it. To an enthusiastic man, his work is always part play, no matter how hard and demanding it is.

F. E. WILLIAMSON

3

Every successful man I have heard of has done the best he could with conditions as he found them, and not waited until the next year for better.

E. W. HOWE

4

Timing is everything. It's as important to know when as to know how.

ARNOLD H. GLASOW

5

It isn't what you know that counts, it's what you think of in time.

LEO AIKMAN

6

Things turn out best for the people who make the best of the way things turn out.

ART LINKLETTER

7

There are no hopeless situations; there are only people who have grown hopeless about them.

CLARE BOOTHE LUCE

8

Vitality shows not only in the ability to persist but in the ability to start over.

F. SCOTT FITZGERALD

9

Both optimists and pessimists contribute to our society. The optimist invents the airplane and the pessimist the parachute.

GIL STERN

10

True happiness comes to him who does his work well, followed by a relaxing and refreshing period of rest. True happiness comes from the right amount of work for the day.

LIN YUTANG

11

Weariness has no pain equal to being all rested up with nothing to do.

HENRY S. HASKINS

12

It's not work that makes you tired. It's frustration that comes from lack of work or lack of accomplishment. Real frustration comes when you cannot find useful work to do.

RICHARD E. HECKERT

13

When I go to bed at night, I ask myself, "Have you done the best job you can do?" If I can say "yes," then I get a good night's sleep and am ready to meet the job the next day.

HARRY S. TRUMAN

14

It's extremely important not to have one's life all blocked out, not to have the days and weeks totally organized. It's essential to leave gaps and interludes for spontaneous action, for it is often in spontaneity and surprises that we open ourselves to the unlimited opportunities and new areas brought into our lives by chance.

JEAN HERSEY

15

Discovery consists of seeing what everybody has seen and thinking what nobody has thought.

ALBERT SZENT-GYÖRGYI

16

Ask someone, "What's half of eight?" Receive the answer, "Zero," and your first reaction is "Nonsense!" But stop a moment. The figure eight is composed of two small zeros piled on top of one another. Take it further. If a line were drawn down the middle of an eight, you would have two threes standing face to face.

By seeing things differently, we can make all kinds of discoveries. We can replace old perceptions with new ones and combine old ideas in new ways, bringing into being something which didn't exist before.

CHRISTOPHER NEWS NOTES

17

There are three children in my family. If they were to confront a spiderweb in the garden, each would react differently. The first child would examine the web and wonder how the spider wove it. The second would worry a great deal about where the spider was at that particular moment. And the third would exclaim, "Oh, look! A trampoline."

One reality, three dimensions.

PHYLLIS THEROUX

18

The main value of travel lies not in where you go but in leaving where you have been. Go to a new place. Have your former gods challenged. Re-examine your axioms. Find out the evidence for your assumptions, and you will with luck begin to set a true value upon the environment from which you came.

I never tire of Sir Oliver Lodge's way of saying this: "The last thing in the world that a deep-sea fish could discover is salt water."

ALAN GREGG, M.D.

19

We know next to nothing about virtually everything. It is not necessary to know the origin of the universe; it is necessary to want to know. Civilization depends not on any particular knowledge, but on the disposition to crave knowledge.

GEORGE F. WILL

20

Just when you think you've graduated from the school of experience, someone thinks up a new course.

MARY H. WALDRIP

21

What we learn with pleasure we never forget.

ALFRED MERCIER

22

Many people go through life committing partial suicide—destroying their talents, energies, creative qualities. To learn how to be good to oneself is often more difficult than to learn how to be good to others.

JOSHUA LOTH LIEBMAN

23

One of the most difficult things to give away is kindness—it is usually returned.

CORT R. FLINT

24

Once in a century a person may be ruined or made insufferable by praise. But surely once in a minute something generous dies for want of it.

JOHN MASEFIELD

25

Encouragement after censure is as the sun after a shower.

JOHANN WOLFGANG VON GOETHE

26

We probably wouldn't worry about what people think of us if we could know how seldom they do.

OLIN MILLER

27

Whether you believe you can do a thing or not, you are right.

HENRY FORD

28

Worry is imagination misplaced.

JIM FIEBIG

29

Creativity is more than just being different. Anybody can play weird; that's easy. What's hard is to be as simple as Bach. Making the simple complicated is commonplace; making the complicated simple, awesomely simple—that's creativity.

CHARLES MINGUS

30

Originality is unexplored territory. You get there by carrying a canoe—you can't take a taxi.

ALAN ALDA

July

1

The advantages of a bad memory: One cannot be a good liar; one cannot tell long stories; one forgets offenses; and one enjoys places and books a second time around.

MONTAIGNE

2

There are three ingredients in the good life: learning, earning and yearning.

CHRISTOPHER MORLEY

3

Better to trust the man who is frequently in error than the one who is never in doubt.

ERIC SEVAREID

4

Almost all our faults are more pardonable than the methods we think up to hide them.

LA ROCHEFOUCAULD

5

He who mistrusts most should be trusted least.

THEOGNIS

6

However much we guard ourselves against it, we tend to shape ourselves in the image others have of us. It is not so much the example of others we imitate, as the reflection of ourselves in their eyes and the echo of ourselves in their words.

ERIC HOFFER

7

One of the best ways to persuade others is with your ears—by listening to them.

DEAN RUSK

8

It's odd how few managers—as well as marriage partners—realize that, if you give way in little things, you can almost always have your way in big ones.

SYDNEY J. HARRIS

9

The difficult part in an argument is not to defend one's opinion but rather to know it.

ANDRÉ MAUROIS

10

Forgiveness is a funny thing. It warms the heart and cools the sting.

WILLIAM ARTHUR WARD

11

An apology is a good way to have the last word.

DELL CROSSWORD PUZZLES

12

Bear in mind that children of all ages have one thing in common—they close their ears to advice and open their eyes to example.

THE TABLET

13

There are good reasons for doing some things fast: because life is crowding in hard, and if the thing isn't done fast it won't be done at all, or because doing it isn't half so rewarding as doing something else. Therefore, iron fast so you can paint slow. Shop fast so you can sew slow. Cook fast so you can spend some time with a child before it disappears into an adult.

PEG BRACKEN

14

If I spent as much time doing the things I worry about getting done as I do worrying about doing them, I wouldn't have anything to worry about.

BERYL PFIZER

15

Chronic remorse is a most undesirable sentiment. If you have behaved badly, repent, make what amends you can, and address yourself to the task of behaving better the next time. On no account brood over your wrongdoing. Rolling in the muck is not the best way of getting clean.

ALDOUS HUXLEY

16

It's done. Finished. Over. There is nothing you can do to change the past. Take heart from the knowledge that something good can come of it if it teaches you a lesson. Profit from it—then forget it.

ANN LANDERS

17

Every man regards his own life as the New Year's Eve of time.

JEAN PAUL RICHTER

18

There are few things more consoling to men than the mere finding that other men have felt as they feel.

FREDERICK W. FABER

19

All mankind is divided into three classes: those who are immovable; those who are movable; and those who move.

BENJAMIN FRANKLIN

20

No horse gets anywhere until he is harnessed. No steam or gas ever drives anything until it is confined. No Niagara is ever turned into light and power until it is tunneled. No life ever grows great until it is focused, dedicated, disciplined.

HARRY EMERSON FOSDICK

21

Keep on going and chances are you will stumble on something, perhaps when you are least expecting it. I have never heard of anyone stumbling on something sitting down.

CHARLES F. KETTERING

22

He who deliberates fully before taking a step will spend his entire life on one leg.

CHINESE PROVERB

23

An opportunist: any person who goes ahead and does what you always intended to do.

KENNETH L. KRICHBAUM

24

We're all in favor of progress, providing we can have it without change.

MORRIE BRICKMAN

25

Too often we enjoy the comfort of opinion without the discomfort of thought.

JOHN F. KENNEDY

26

Don't be afraid to take a big step if one is indicated. You can't cross a chasm in two small jumps.

DAVID LLOYD GEORGE

27

God grant me the serenity
To accept the things I cannot change,
The courage to change the things I can,
And the wisdom to know the difference.

AUTHOR UNKNOWN

28

Man alone, of all the creatures of earth, can change his own pattern. Man alone is architect of his destiny.

WILFERD A. PETERSON

29

More good things in life are lost by indifference than ever were lost by active hostility.

ROBERT GORDON MENZIES

30

To know what is right and not to do it is the worst cowardice.

CONFUCIUS

31

I long to accomplish a great and noble task, but it is my chief duty to accomplish small tasks as if they were great and noble. Green, the historian, tells us that the world is moved along, not only by the mighty shoves of its heroes, but also by the aggregate of the tiny pushes of each honest worker.

HELEN KELLER

August

1

It is not the lofty sails but the unseen wind that moves the ship.

W. MACNEILE DIXON

2

The smallest deed is better than the grandest intention.

LARRY EISENBERG

3

Our main business is not to see what lies dimly at a distance, but to do what lies clearly at hand.

THOMAS CARLYLE

4

Take things as they come. But try to make things come as you would like to take them.

CURT GOETZ

5

Not everything that is faced can be changed. But nothing can be changed until it is faced.

JAMES BALDWIN

6

"I must do something" will always solve more problems than "Something must be done."

BITS & PIECES

7

The desk motto we like best reads: "Right now is a good time."

GERALD HORTON BATH

8

He who cannot change the very fabric of his thought will never be able to change reality.

ANWAR EL-SADAT

9

The chief danger in life is that you may take too many precautions.

ALFRED ADLER

10

You only live once. But if you work it right, once is enough.

FRED ALLEN

11

If you're never scared or embarrassed or hurt, it means you never take any chances.

JULIA SOREL

12

You don't become a better person because you are suffering; but you become a better person because you have experienced suffering. We can't appreciate light if we haven't known darkness. Nor can we appreciate warmth if we have never suffered cold. It's not what you've lost that's important. What is important is what you have left.

CHRISTIAAN N. BARNARD, M.D.

13

Live always as if there is world enough and time.

EXECUTIVE HEALTH REPORT

14

Don't put off for tomorrow what you can do today, because if you enjoy it today you can do it again tomorrow.

JAMES A. MICHENER

15

People relate to time in many different ways. Referees call *time; prisoners* serve *time; musicians* mark *time; historians* record *time; loafers* kill *time; statisticians* keep *time. But no matter how people relate to time, the fact remains that all of us are given the same amount of time. There are only 24 hours per day, 168 hours per week. Use them.*

DENNIS HENSLEY

16

Not keeping an appointment is an act of clear dishonesty. You may as well borrow a person's money as his time.

HORACE MANN

17

The most important thing in life is not simply to capitalize on your gains. Any fool can do that. The important thing is to profit from your losses. That requires intelligence, and it makes the difference between a person of sense and a fool.

WILLIAM BOLITHO

18

Someone who thinks the world is always cheating him is right—he is missing that wonderful feeling of trust in someone or something.

ANDREW V. MASON, M.D.

19

You may find the worst enemy or best friend in yourself.

ENGLISH PROVERB

20

True contentment is the power of getting out of any situation all that there is in it.

G. K. CHESTERTON

21

The highest reward for man's toil is not what he gets for it but what he becomes by it.

JOHN RUSKIN

22

Everybody thinks of changing humanity and nobody thinks of changing himself.

LEO TOLSTOY

23

Self-discipline is when your conscience tells you to do something and you don't talk back.

W. K. HOPE

24

The only person who behaves sensibly is my tailor. He takes my measure anew every time he sees me. All the rest go on with their old measurements.

BERNARD SHAW

25

The true test of intelligence is not how much we know how to do, but how we behave when we don't know what to do.

JOHN HOLT

26

You are not mature until you expect the unexpected.

CHICAGO *TRIBUNE*

27

The older I grow, the more I listen to people who don't talk much.

GERMAIN G. GLIDDEN

28

Success is often the result of taking a misstep in the right direction.

AL BERNSTEIN

29

Sign in an executive's office: "What I am about to say represents one four-billionth of the world's opinion."

JACK WILLIAMS

30

Keep your fears to yourself, but share your courage.

ROBERT LOUIS STEVENSON

31

The superior man is distressed by the limitations of his ability; he is not distressed by the fact that men do not recognize the ability he has.

CONFUCIUS

September

1

Let the other fellow find out who you are. He'll remember it longer.

THE WALL STREET JOURNAL

2

Trying to impress others does—usually in quite the opposite way.

MALCOLM S. FORBES

3

Young people searching for their "real self" must learn that the real self is not something one finds as much as it is something one makes; and it is one's daily actions that shape the inner personality far more permanently than any amount of introspection or intellection.

SYDNEY J. HARRIS

4

One does not "find oneself" by pursuing one's self, but on the contrary by pursuing something else and learning through discipline or routine—even the routine of making beds—who one is and wants to be.

MAY SARTON

5

A man cannot be comfortable without his own approval.

MARK TWAIN

6

I don't wait for moods. You accomplish nothing if you do that. Your mind must know it has got to get down to work.

PEARL BUCK

7

Discipline is like broccoli. We may not care for it ourselves, but feel sure it would be good for everybody else.

BILL VAUGHAN

8

Besides the noble art of getting things done, there is the noble art of leaving things undone. The wisdom of life consists in the elimination of non-essentials.

LIN YUTANG

9

Next to knowing when to seize an opportunity, the most important thing in life is to know when to forego an advantage.

BENJAMIN DISRAELI

10

A hunch is creativity trying to tell you something.

FRANK CAPRA

11

The trouble with not having a goal is that you can spend your life running up and down the field and never scoring.

BILL COPELAND

12

If you have built castles in the air, your work need not be lost: that is where they should be. Now put the foundations under them.

HENRY D. THOREAU

13

The best way to make your dreams come true is to wake up.

J. M. POWER

14

I have had dreams, and I have had nightmares. I overcame the nightmares because of my dreams.

JONAS SALK, M.D.

15

Most of us could move mountains if only someone would clear the foothills out of the way.

BOB TALBERT

16

The defect of equality is that we desire it only with our superiors.

HENRY BECQUE

17

The most beaten paths are certainly the surest; but do not hope to scare up much game on them.

ANDRÉ GIDE

18

The wishbone will never replace the backbone.

WILL HENRY

19

Success is often just an idea away.

FRANK TYGER

20

Words without ideas are like sails without wind.

BLACKSTONE, VA., *COURIER-RECORD*

21

At first it is difficult to recognize an idea as original. Nearly any notion, whether old, banal, spurious, novel or brilliant, may pop up with a flutter of excitement. How is one to distinguish? Notice, after three days, whether it still quivers.

KENNETH A. FISHER

22

Bring ideas in and entertain them royally, for one of them may be the king.

MARK VAN DOREN

23

The test of a first-rate intelligence is the ability to hold two opposed ideas in the mind at the same time, and still retain the ability to function.

F. SCOTT FITZGERALD

24

Everything has been thought of before, but the difficulty is to think of it again.

JOHANN WOLFGANG VON GOETHE

25

One who never asks knows either everything or nothing.

MALCOLM S. FORBES

26

Let us not be arrogant toward the ignorant—their sensitivity is often too deep to dare the knowledge of numbers or the curlicue within a letter. Picasso, age of 11, could still not do arithmetic because the figure 7 looked to him like a nose upside down.

NORMAN MAILER

27

The trouble with doing something right the first time is that nobody appreciates how difficult it was.

AL BERNSTEIN

28

One of the greatest sources of energy is pride in what you are doing.

SPOKES

29

There is no comparison between that which is lost by not succeeding and that which is lost by not trying.

FRANCIS BACON

30

If at first you don't succeed, try, try again. Then give up. There's no use in being a darn fool about it.

W. C. FIELDS

October

1

When making a decision of minor importance, I have always found it advantageous to consider all the pros and cons. In vital matters, however, such as the choice of a mate or a profession, the decision should come from the unconscious. The important decisions of our personal life should be governed by the deep inner needs of our nature.

SIGMUND FREUD

2

I have never met a person who has given me as much trouble as myself.

DWIGHT L. MOODY

3

Opportunities are never lost. The other fellow takes those you miss.

AUTHOR UNKNOWN

4

If you can find a path with no obstacles, it probably doesn't lead anywhere.

FRANK A. CLARK

5

You can't build a reputation on what you are going to do.

HENRY FORD

6

Opportunity is sometimes hard to recognize if you're only looking for a lucky break.

MONTA CRANE

7

Some people have all the luck. And they're the ones who never depend on it.

BOB INGHAM

8

The only thing sure about luck is that it will change.

BRET HARTE

9

Progress is not created by contented people.

FRANK TYGER

10

Success does for living what sunshine does for stained glass.

BOB TALBERT

11

I have three precious things which I hold fast and prize. The first is gentleness; the second is frugality; the third is humility, which keeps me from putting myself before others. Be gentle and you can be bold; be frugal and you can be liberal; avoid putting yourself before others, and you can become a leader among men.

LAO-TSE

12

You can't expect a person to see eye to eye with you when you're looking down on him.

BITS & PIECES

13

A person who enjoys responsibility usually gets it. A person who merely likes exercising authority usually loses it.

MALCOLM S. FORBES

14

Few things help an individual more than to place responsibility upon him and to let him know that you trust him.

BOOKER T. WASHINGTON

15

Never tell people how to do things. Tell them what to do and they will surprise you with their ingenuity.

GEN. GEORGE S. PATTON, JR.

16

People learn something every day, and a lot of times it's that what they learned the day before was wrong.

BILL VAUGHAN

17

Strong people make as many and as ghastly mistakes as weak people. The difference is that strong people admit them, laugh at them, learn from them. That is how they became strong.

RICHARD J. NEEDHAM

18

A letter from a reader to "Dear Abby" posed the following question: "I wondered why somebody didn't do something. Then I realized I was somebody."

CHICAGO TRIBUNE—N.Y. NEWS SYNDICATE

19

The man who rows the boat seldom has time to rock it.

BILL COPELAND

20

When you have to make a choice and don't make it, that is in itself a choice.

WILLIAM JAMES

21

There are those who are so scrupulously afraid of doing wrong that they seldom venture to do anything.

VAUVENARGUES

22

The haves and the have-nots can often be traced back to the dids and the did-nots.

D. O. FLYNN

23

Think of what you have rather than of what you lack. Of the things you have, select the best and then reflect how eagerly you would have sought them if you did not have them.

MARCUS AURELIUS

24

The misfortunes hardest to bear are those which never happen.

JAMES RUSSELL LOWELL

25

That some good can be derived from every event is a better proposition than that everything happens for the best, which it assuredly does not.

JAMES K. FEIBLEMAN

26

People in distress will sometimes prefer a problem that is familiar to a solution that is not.

NEIL POSTMAN

27

An hour's industry will do more to produce cheerfulness, suppress evil humors and retrieve your affairs than a month's moaning.

BENJAMIN FRANKLIN

28

One half of life is luck; the other half is discipline—and that's the important half, for without discipline you wouldn't know what to do with your luck.

CARL ZUCKMAYER

29

Discipline is the refining fire by which talent becomes ability.

ROY L. SMITH

30

A genius is one who shoots at something no one else can see, and hits it.

THE LUTHERAN DIGEST

31

Genius is recognizing the uniqueness in the unimpressive. It is looking at a homely caterpillar, an ordinary egg and a selfish infant, and seeing a butterfly, an eagle and a saint.

WILLIAM ARTHUR WARD

November

1

Leaves are like ideas in the mind. They come when needed. They flourish and give life, light and wisdom. When ideas have served their purpose, they need to be swept away. We must constantly sweep out the old to make way for the new.

JAN MCKEITHEN

2

Every conviction was a whim at birth.

HEYWOOD BROUN

3

He who truly knows has no occasion to shout.

LEONARDO DA VINCI

4

If you wouldn't write it and sign it, don't say it.

EARL WILSON

5

The hardest thing to learn in life is which bridge to cross and which to burn.

DAVID RUSSELL

6

It's so much easier to suggest solutions when you don't know too much about the problem.

MALCOLM S. FORBES

7

Sometimes a majority simply means that all the fools are on the same side.

CLAUDE MCDONALD

8

Asking "Who ought to be boss?" is like saying "Who ought to be the tenor in the quartet?" Obviously, the man who can sing tenor.

HENRY FORD

9

Frustration is commonly the difference between what you would like to be and what you are willing to sacrifice to become what you would like to be.

SYDNEY J. HARRIS

10

How often we are offended by not being offered something we do not really want.

ERIC HOFFER

11

Were we to take as much pains to be what we ought, as we do to disguise what we are, we might appear like ourselves without being at the trouble of any disguise at all.

LA ROCHEFOUCAULD

12

Trying to squash a rumor is like trying to unring a bell.

SHANA ALEXANDER

13

A great lie is like a great fish on dry land: it may fret and fling and make a frightful bother, but it cannot hurt you. You have only to keep still, and it will die of itself.

GEORGE CRABBE

14

A long habit of not thinking a thing wrong gives it a superficial appearance of being right.

THOMAS PAINE

15

When a man says he approves of something in principle, it means he hasn't the slightest intention of putting it into practice.

OTTO VON BISMARCK

16

The ideal committee consists of two, four or six people who haven't time, and one person who likes to run things his own way.

KEARNEY HUB

17

If you ask enough people, you can usually find someone who'll advise you to do what you were going to do anyway.

WESTON SMITH

18

How can you tell if you really want to do something? Toss a coin. *Literally. It works—not because it settles the question for you, but, as the Danish poet and mathematician Piet Hein said, while the coin is in the air, "You suddenly know what you're hoping."*

MADELINE LEE

19

My idea of an agreeable person is a person who agrees with me.

BENJAMIN DISRAELI

20

We may not return the affection of those who like us, but we always respect their good judgment.

LIBBIE FUDIM

21

We are never more discontented with others than when we are discontented with ourselves.

HENRI FREDERIC AMIEL

22

The most difficult thing in the world is to know how to do a thing and to watch somebody else doing it wrong, without comment.

T. H. WHITE

23

The kindest word in all the world is the unkind word, unsaid.

OFFICIAL CROSSWORD PUZZLES

24

For peace of mind, resign as general manager of the universe.

LARRY EISENBERG

25

Deceiving someone for his own good is a responsibility that should be shouldered only by the gods.

HENRY S. HASKINS

26

Our faults irritate us most when we see them in others.

PENNSYLVANIA DUTCH PROVERB

27

Nothing so needs reforming as other people's habits.

MARK TWAIN

28

I have yet to be bored by someone paying me a compliment.

OTTO VAN ISCH

29

With money in your pocket, you are wise and you are handsome and you sing well, too.

YIDDISH PROVERB

30

What's in a word? Consider the difference between wise guy and wise man.

MARSHALLTOWN, IOWA, *TIMES-REPUBLICAN*

December

1

There's nothing so annoying as arguing with a person who knows what he's talking about.

VOICE FOR HEALTH

2

Facts do not cease to exist because they are ignored.

ALDOUS HUXLEY

3

Crowding a life does not always enrich it.

ROSE KENNEDY

4

Excess on occasion is exhilarating. It prevents moderation from acquiring the deadening effect of a habit.

SOMERSET MAUGHAM

5

Have you noticed that even the busiest people are never too busy to take time to tell you how busy they are?

BOB TALBERT

6

No one really listens to anyone else. Try it for a while, and you'll see why.

MIGNON MCLAUGHLIN

7

The most valuable of all talents is that of never using two words when one will do.

THOMAS JEFFERSON

8

The real art of conversation is not only to say the right thing in the right place but to leave unsaid the wrong thing at the tempting moment.

DOROTHY NEVILL

9

It's all right to hold a conversation, but you should let go of it now and then.

RICHARD ARMOUR

10

For good or ill, your conversation is your advertisement. Every time you open your mouth you let others look into your mind.

BRUCE BARTON

11

It is harder to conceal ignorance than to acquire knowledge.

ARNOLD H. GLASOW

12

Never claim as a right what you can ask as a favor.

JOHN CHURTON COLLINS

13

Influence is like a savings account. The less you use it, the more you've got.

ANDREW YOUNG

14

Don't be troubled if the temptation to give advice is irresistible; the ability to ignore it is universal.

PLANNED FINANCIAL SECURITY

15

To be exactly the opposite is also a form of imitation.

GEORG C. LICHTENBERG

16

The way to gain a good reputation is to endeavor to be what you desire to appear.

SOCRATES

17

On an open mind: it ought not to be so open that there is no keeping anything in or out of it. It should be capable of shutting its doors, or it may be found a little drafty.

SAMUEL BUTLER

18

Nothing lowers the level of conversation more than raising the voice.

STANLEY HOROWITZ

19

Everything becomes a little different as soon as it is spoken out loud.

HERMANN HESSE

20

An elderly woman asked Abraham Lincoln, "How can you speak kindly of your enemies when you should rather destroy them?" "Madam," he said, "do I not destroy them when I make them my friends?"

CARL SANDBURG

21

Too many people don't care what happens so long as it doesn't happen to them.

WILLIAM HOWARD TAFT

22

Sometimes the best way to convince someone he is wrong is to let him have his way.

RED O'DONNELL

23

Few things are harder to put up with than the annoyance of a good example.

MARK TWAIN

24

More people are flattered into virtue than are bullied out of vice.

ROBERT SMITH SURTEES

25

Each day comes bearing its gifts, untie the ribbons.

ANN RUTH SCHABACKER

26

There is only one world, the world pressing against you at this minute. There is only one minute in which you are alive, this minute—here and now. The only way to live is by accepting each minute as an unrepeatable miracle. Which is exactly what it is—a miracle and unrepeatable.

STORM JAMESON

27

Yesterday is a canceled check; tomorrow is a promissory note; today is ready cash—use it.

KAY LYONS

28

If you realize that you aren't as wise today as you thought you were yesterday, you're wiser today.

BULLETIN OF DETROIT JEFFERSON AVENUE PRESBYTERIAN CHURCH

29

There are nine requisites for contented living: health enough to make work a pleasure; wealth enough to support your needs; strength to battle with difficulties and overcome them; grace enough to confess your sins and forsake them; patience enough to toil until some good is accomplished; charity enough to see some good in your neighbor; love enough to move you to be useful and helpful to others; faith enough to make real the things of God; hope enough to remove all anxious fears concerning the future.

JOHANN WOLFGANG VON GOETHE

30

Our imagination is the only limit to what we can hope to have in the future.

CHARLES F. KETTERING

31

People are unreasonable, illogical and self-centered.
Love them anyway.
If you do good, people will accuse you of selfish ulterior motives.
Do good anyway.
If you are successful, you will win false friends and true enemies.
Succeed anyway.
Honesty and frankness make you vulnerable.
Be honest and frank anyway.
The good you do today will be forgotten tomorrow.
Do good anyway.
The biggest people with the biggest ideas can be shot down by the smallest people with the smallest minds.
Think big anyway.
People favor underdogs but follow only top dogs.
Fight for some underdogs anyway.
What you spend years building may be destroyed overnight.
Build anyway.
Give the world the best you have and you'll get kicked in the teeth.
Give the world the best you've got anyway.

RESPONSE

ACKNOWLEDGMENTS

Grateful acknowledgment is made to the following organizations and individuals for permission to reprint.

Loudon Wainwright in Life; J.B. Priestley; William Allen White in *A Treasury of Contentment*, edited by Ralph L. Woods (Trident); *The Journal of Jules Renard*, edited by Louise Bogan (Braziller); Bonnie Prudden; *A Touch of Wonder* by Arthur Gordon. Copyright © 1974 by Fleming H. Revell Company. Used by permission; Will Henry, Chicago Tribune-New York News Syndicate; *Choice of Pearls* by Solomon Ibn Gabirol (Bloch Publishing Co.); Elizabeth Kübler-Ross in *To Live and to Die*, edited by Robert H. Williams (Springer-Verlag New York); François Mauriac; Thomas L. Masson, *The Best Stories in the World* (Doubleday); Robert H. Schuller; Bob Goddard in St. Louis Globe-Democrat; From *Up The Organization*, by Robert Townsend. Copyright © 1970 by Robert Townsend. Reprinted by permission of Alfred A. Knopf, Inc.; Doug Larson, United Feature Syndicate; Sinclair Lewis, *Main Street* (Harcourt Brace Jovanovich); *The Lives of a Cell* by Lewis Thomas. Copyright © 1974 by Lewis Thomas. Reprinted by permission of Viking Penguin, Inc.; Copyright 1920 by Alfred A. Knopf, Inc. and renewed 1948 by J. Middleton Murry. Reprinted from *The Short Stories of Katherine Mansfield*, by Katherine Mansfield, by permission of the publisher; Beryl Pfizer in Ladies' Home Journal. Copyright © 1972 by Downe Publishing Co., Inc. Reprinted by special permission of the Ladies' Home Journal; Paul Harvey. Copyright © 1964 by Los Angeles Times Syndicate. Reprinted with permission; Robert Haven Schauffler in The Atlantic Monthly; Anatole France.

Sydney J. Harris, Field Newspaper Syndicate; Eda LeShan in Woman's Day. Copyright © 1980 by Eda LeShan; *Look Eleven Years Younger* by Gelett Burgess (Simon & Schuster); Wilferd A. Peterson; Franklin P. Jones in The Wall Street Journal; Farmer's Digest; Funny Funny World; Leo Aikman in Atlanta Constitution; Mark Van Doren; Bruce Barton; Joan L. Brannon; Konrad Adenauer; Cicely Tyson in New Woman Magazine; Rev. Canon M.A. Hughes in Dialogue; *Personal Power Through Creative Selling* by Elmer G. Leterman. Copyright © 1955 by Elmer G. Leterman. Reprinted by permission of Harper & Row, Publishers, Inc.; Fredelle Maynard in Woman's Day.

How To Be Your Own Best Friend by Mildred Newman and Bernard Berkowitz with Jean Owen. Copyright © 1971 by Mildred Newman and Bernard Berkowitz. Reprinted by permission of Random House, Inc.; Henry Mitchell in Washington Post; Grit Publishing Co.; Dr. Alexander G. Bearn; *Minister's Shop-Talk* by James W. Kennedy. Copyright © 1965 by James W. Kennedy. Reprinted by permission of Harper & Row, Publishers, Inc.; Frank Outlaw in Sunshine Magazine; *Your Erroneous Zones* by Wayne W. Dyer.

Copyright © 1976 by Wayne W. Dyer (Harper & Row, Publishers, Inc.); Bill Gove, quoted in *The Fine Art of Doing Better*, edited by D. John Hammond (American Motivational Association); *Nobody Knows My Name* by James Baldwin (The Dial Press); *I Ain't Much, Baby—But I'm All I've Got* by Jess Lair (Doubleday); Quotation by Walter Russell Bowie is reprinted from *On Being Alive* with the permission of Charles Scribner's Sons. Copyright 1931 by Charles Scribner's Sons, copyright renewed 1959 by Walter Russell Bowie; Dubois County, Ind., Herald; Alfred Rice, Trustee, Estate of Ernest Hemingway; *The Season of the Witch* by James Leo Herlihy. Copyright © 1971 by James Leo Herlihy (Simon & Schuster); Billy Graham, Chicago Tribune-New York News Syndicate; Duncan Stuart, quoted by Gerald Horton Bath in The Little Gazette; Sylvia Robinson in The Christian Science Monitor; G. K. Chesterton; Leo Rosten; Charles F. Kettering Foundation; Will Rogers. Holbrook Jackson in Ladies' Home Journal; Dwight D. Eisenhower in The Saturday Evening Post; Ann Landers, Field Newspaper Syndicate; Jessamyn

West; Elbert Hubbard II; Arnold Glasow in The Wall Street Journal; Sacha Guitry; Bob Talbert in Detroit Free Press; *Economics, Peace and Laughter* by John Kenneth Galbraith, edited by Andrea D. Williams (Houghton Mifflin); Hal Chadwick; Malcolm S. Forbes in Forbes Magazine; Bill Copeland in Sarasota, Fla., Journal; Katherine Chandler, quoted by Red O'Donnell in Nashville Banner; *Fountains of Faith* by William Arthur Ward (Drake House Publishers, Inc.); W. A. Nance in Holiday Inn Magazine; Joseph P. Kennedy, Jr. Foundation; *Mr. Citizen* by Harry S. Truman (Bernard Geis Associates, Inc.); The Better Way (House of Sunshine); Jim Goodwin in Graham, Texas, Rotary "Scandal Sheet"; Libbie Fudim; Marie Curie.

Dorothy Van Doren; Charles Barsotti in Long Island, N.Y. Newsday; Marya Mannes in McCall's; *How to Stop Worrying and Start Living* by Dale Carnegie (Simon & Schuster); Christiaan N. Barnard, M.D.; *To See the Dream* © 1956, 1957 by Jessamyn West. Reprinted with permission of Harcourt Brace Jovanovich, Inc.; Don Herold; Judge Shirley M. Hufstedler quoted by Marshall Berges in Los Angeles Times; From the book *Relax and Live* by Joseph A. Kennedy. © 1953 by Joseph A. Kennedy. Published by Prentice-Hall, Inc.; Franklin P. Jones in Quote; Reprinted from *The Secret of Staying in Love* by John Powell. © 1974 Argus Communications. Used with permission from Argus Communications, One DLM Park, Allen, TX 75002; Robert Morley; Frank Tyger in Graham, Texas, Rotary "Scandal Sheet"; *Quotations of Courage and Vision*, edited by Carl Hermann Voss (Association Press); Earl Wilson, Field Newspaper Syndicate; *Afterthoughts* by Logan Pearsall Smith (Harcourt Brace Jovanovich); John Raudonis, quoted by Hugh Park in Atlanta Journal-Constitution; From *Katherine Mansfield's Letters to John Middleton Murry 1913-1922*, by Katherine Mansfield. Copyright 1929, 1951 by Alfred A. Knopf, Inc. and renewed by J. Middleton Murry. Reprinted by permission of the publisher; Danny Thomas, quoted by Kay Gardella in New York Daily News; Helen Hayes in Bits & Pieces; Earl Nightingale; Norman Lear, quoted by Marguerite Michaels in Parade; Carl Sandburg, quoted by Ralph McGill, Field Newspaper Syndicate; Reverend Jesse L. Jackson; Dr. Heinrich Sobotka in Madame, Germany.

Alex Noble; F. E. Williamson in The American Magazine; E. W. Howe in Forbes Magazine; Art Linkletter, quoted by Tony Stein in Norfolk Ledger-Star; Claire Boothe Luce in Sunshine Magazine; F. Scott Fitzgerald in *The Crack-up*, edited by Edmund Wilson (New Directions); Gil Stern in Chicago Tribune; Lin Yutang; *Meditations In Wall Street* by Henry S. Haskins (Morrow); Richard E. Heckert; From *The Touch of the Earth* by Jean Hersey. Copyright © 1981 by Jean Hersey. Used by permission of The Seabury Press, Inc.; Albert Szent-Gÿorgi in Scope®, The Upjohn Company, Kalamazoo, MI; Christopher News Notes; Phyllis Theroux in New York Times. © 1979 by The New York Times Company. Reprinted by permission; *For Future Doctors* by Alan Gregg, M.D. (University of Chicago Press); George F. Will in Newsweek; Mary H. Waldrip in Dawson County, Ga., Advertiser and News; *Peace of Mind* by Joshua Loth Liebman (Simon & Schuster); Cort R. Flint in Quote Magazine; John Masefield; Olin Miller; Henry Ford; Jim Fiebig, North American Newspaper Alliance; Charles Mingus, quoted by Franz Lidz in Sports Illustrated; Alan Alda in foreword to M*A*S*H by David S. Reiss (Bobbs-Merrill).

Christopher Morley; Eric Sevareid, CBS News; Eric Hoffer quoted in Forbes Magazine; Dean Rusk; *The Art of Living* by André Maurois (Harper & Row); Dell Crossword Puzzles; The Tablet; *I Hate to Cook Almanack* by Peg Bracken (Harcourt Brace Jovanovich); *Brave New World* by Aldous Huxley (Harper & Row); Excerpt from *The Ann Landers Encyclopedia A-Z* by Ann Landers. Copyright © 1978 by Esther P. Lederer. Reprinted by permission of Doubleday

& Co. Inc.; *Living Under Tension* by Harry Emerson Fosdick (Harper & Row); Kenneth L. Krichbaum in The Saturday Evening Post; from "small society" by Morrie Brickman, King Features Syndicate, Inc.; Robert Gordon Menzies; Helen Keller International Inc.
The Human Situation by W. MacNeile Dixon (Edward Arnold Ltd.); *Bulletin Boarders* by Larry Eisenberg (C.S.S. Publishing); *Four Times Daily* by Curt Goetz © 1968 by Valerie Von Martens-Goetz, Schaan/Liechtenstein, by courtesy of Deutsche Verlags-Anstalt GMBH, Stuttgart; James Baldwin; Bits & Pieces; *In Search of Identity* by Anwar el-Sadat (Harper & Row); Alfred Adler; Fred Allen; From *See How She Runs*, by Julia Sorel. Copyright © 1978 by Marvin Gluck c/o Major Talent Agency, Inc. Reprinted by permission of Ballantine Books, a Division of Random House, Inc.; Executive Health Report; From *The Drifters* by James A. Michener. Copyright © 1971 by Random House, Inc. Reprinted by permission of the publisher; Dennis Hensley in Writer's Digest; William Bolitho, quoted by Dale Carnegie, *How to Stop Worrying and Start Living* (Simon & Schuster); *Surgeon's Log* by Andrew V. Mason, M.D. (Christopher Publishing House); W. K. Hope. © 1981 by The Reader's Digest Association, Inc.; Bernard Shaw in *Man and Superman;* Excerpted from the book *How Children Fail* Revised Edition by John Holt. Copyright © 1964, 1982 by John Holt. Reprinted by permission of Delacorte Press/Seymour Lawrence. A Merloyd Lawrence Book; Chicago Tribune; Germain G. Glidden; Al Bernstein in Chicago Tribune; Jack Williams in Phoenix Gazette.
The Wall Street Journal; *The House by the Sea* by May Sarton (Norton); *What Is Man? and Other Essays* by Mark Twain (Harper & Row); Pearl Buck in Your Life; Bill Vaughan in Kansas City Star; *On the Wisdom of America* by Lin Yutang (John Day); Frank Capra on "Mike Douglas Show," Group W. Productions; J. M. Power in Sign Magazine; Jonas Salk, M.D.; Bob Talbert in Detroit Free Press; André Gide; Will Henry, Chicago Tribune–New York News Syndicate; Frank Tyger in Forbes Magazine; Blackstone, Va., Courier-Record; *The Guru Therapist's Notebook* by Kenneth A. Fisher (Adelphi University Press); Norman Mailer in The New York Times Magazine. © 1969 by The New York Times Company. Reprinted by permission; Spokes; W. C. Fields.
Sigmund Freud, quoted by Theodor Reik in *Listening With the Third Ear* (Farrar, Straus & Giroux); Frank A. Clark, Register and Tribune Syndicate; Monta Crane in Joys of Life; *War As I Knew It* by Gen. George S. Patton, Jr. (Houghton Mifflin); *The Wit & Wisdom of Richard Needham* by Richard J. Needham (Hurtig, Canada); D. O. Flynn in The Saturday Evening Post; *The Way of a Man* by James K. Feibleman (Horizon Press); Neil Postman in The New York Times Magazine. © 1972 by The New York Times Company. Reprinted by permission; Carl Zuckmayer, quoted by Janik Press Service; *Splinters* by Roy L. Smith (Fleming H. Revell); The Lutheran Digest; William Arthur Ward in Quote Magazine.
Jan McKeithen in Camden County, Ga., Tribune; Heywood Broun; David Russell, quoted by Laurence J. Peter in *The Peter Plan* (Morrow); *The Sayings of Chairman Malcolm* by Malcolm Forbes (Harper & Row); Claude McDonald in The Christian Word; *My Life and Work* by Henry Ford (Doubleday); *Reflections on the Human Condition* by Eric Hoffer (Harper & Row); *Anyone's Daughter* by Shana Alexander (Viking); Kearney Hub; Weston Smith,quoted in Funny Funny World; Madeline Lee; T. H. White in Atlantic Monthly; Official Crossword Puzzles; Otto Van Isch, quoted by Earl Wilson, Field Newspaper Syndicate; Marshalltown, Iowa, Times-Republican.
Voice for Health; *Proper Studies* by Aldous Huxley (Harper & Row); From the notebook of Rose Kennedy, quoted by Laura Berquist in Look (Cowles Broadcasting, Inc.); *Summing Up* by Somerset Maugham (Doubleday); Mignon

McLaughlin; *Under Five Reigns* by Dorothy Nevill (Methuen); Richard Armour, quoted in The Saturday Evening Post; Andrew Young, quoted in People; Planned Financial Security; *Behind the Glass* by Stanley Horowitz (Horowitz); Herman Hesse; *Abraham Lincoln* by Carl Sandburg (Harcourt Brace Jovanovich); Red O'Donnell in Nashville Banner; Ann Ruth Schabacker in The Christian Science Monitor; Storm Jameson in This Week Magazine; Kay Lyons in The Catholic News of Western New York; Bulletin of Detroit Jefferson Avenue Presbyterian Church; Response, Bulletin of Presbyterian Church of White Plains.

Book design by Vicky-Jean Taloni

Cover design by Patrice Barrett

Cover photograph by Freelance Photographers Guild, Inc.

Book type set in Melior Italic and Bold; Cover type set in Romic